Responding to Callers

A Guide to Doorstep Care

John Hall

Vicar of St Aldhelm, Edmonton, London and
formerly Senior Probation Officer

GROVE BOOKS LIMITED
RIDLEY HALL RD CAMBRIDGE CB3 9HU

Contents

1. Introduction 3
2. The Callers 3
3. Models for Care and Key Issues 6
4. Theology and the Provision of Care 11
5. Care in Practice 15
6. Care for Carers 18
7. Limits of Care 20
Appendix: Guidelines for Practice 23

The Cover Illustration is by Peter Ashton

Copyright © John Hall 1999

First Impression September 1999
ISSN 0144-171X
ISBN 1 85174 412 6

1
Introduction

You are the caller
You are the poor
You are the stranger at my door...
You are the other who comes to me
If I open to another you are born in me.

David Adam

People in need and on the street come to churches hoping to find love. They might not put it in those terms, but Christians are still seen as those who will be kind, even to strangers, 24 hours a day. Knocking at the door of the church, the church office or the clergy residence, people in need present themselves for help. They are the callers at our door; we who answer are those called to care.

In London and in towns and cities up and down the land, people who call usually ask for money, food and drink. At my vicarage door in London we have on average at least one caller a week. London churches receive an average of more than 15 callers a week; in other places the number is usually smaller. But unless the church is off the beaten track, people will call at the door. Every single person who calls matters—as do those who care for them.

This booklet is about the care of the caller and those called upon to help. This ministry is not just the responsibility of the minister or church worker alone, but concerns the whole church congregation, its governing committees and training personnel.

2
The Callers

For the most part the encounter of someone coming to the door is incident free and callers go away grateful for the help even though all that they requested may not have been granted. However, the doorstep encounter is not always without incident. Let us begin with a couple of true stories:

- *Steve* is not yet 30. He came to the door asking for food but it was not a good time as the vicar was out and the vicar's wife was busy. Of necessity, she could only give him some of the tins of food that had been kept back from harvest festival for just such a need. Steve did not like what he was given and became aggressive. Locking the children inside, the vicar's wife ran to the church next door to call for help. The vicar sensed danger and went to deal with the new emergency.

The caller was dirty and stinking, his matted beard green and white from the mucous discharging from his nose. As the vicar accompanied Steve back toward the vicarage, the man took one of the tins of food, placed it on the vicarage front-door step and stamped on it heavily. Fruit cocktail went everywhere. He did likewise with the other tins, sending a shower of disgorged food every few yards. Finally he hurled the bag of the remaining tins in the path of an oncoming bus. He made off down the road, annoying motorists as he shouted at them angrily.

Steve had called before for help. When would he call next, and what would he do then?

- *Gary* was not long out of prison. It was teatime, the week before Christmas, and the vicarage children were home from school, waiting to be fed. The vicar answered the knock at his door and saw a young man who was unsteady on his feet, yet tall, muscular and menacing. When the visitor demanded money, the vicar cautiously asked what he needed it for, secretly thinking that it would buy yet more drink. Gary said angrily that it was for food.

  Closing the door and leaving Gary on the step, the vicar disappeared inside to make up a pack of sandwiches to give Gary along with other supplies. But when they were handed to Gary, he responded not with 'thank you,' but with a sudden outburst of violent and abusive behaviour. Uttering expletives, he forcefully threw the food at the vicarage before leaving, hitting the metal railings of the church as he went and threatening the vicar not to call the police. Having heard all that went on, one of the vicarage children became too frightened to leave the house during the following week for fear of the man.

- *Sue*, a wife of a clergyman, lives in constant fear. She only answers the door with a dog beside her. Their walled garden now has barbed wire on top; heavy metal gates provide the only access to the house. The solid wooden front doors have a chain, peep hole and metal bolts. Unbreakable glass has been installed in the windows.

  Strangers are only admitted when two adults are present and the children are not allowed to open the door without seeing who is outside first. Babysitters have to be able to cope with the security system before they can be allowed to mind the children. The downstairs is alarmed each night and outside flood lights have been installed. Beside the phone for the next emergency are the numbers for the churchwardens and police. Because of where they live, Sue is constantly frightened.

THE CALLERS

Life in London
I could draw on many similar stories from my seven years in this parish. And other clergy and church workers have their stories too; in recent years some have been subjected to violence and even on occasion killed or injured. Thankfully, this is rare, but long gone are the days when the stranger calling for help was a fairly amiable gentleman of the road asking for a 'cuppa tea' or volunteering to sweep up leaves for a 'couple of bob.' Though a few such characters still exist, they are now the exception rather than the rule and the caller of today is an altogether much more challenging proposition. It is not unusual for the caller at the door to request way beyond what most of us have the ability to cope with, though often we may not be prepared to admit this.

As a vicar in London, several miles north of the Waterloo Bridge and the Embankment that many hundreds of street dwellers call home, I often find callers in need of care at the door of the vicarage or church office. They are generally young people asking for or even demanding money; more often than not they are hungry and thirsty. Sometimes they are cold and lonely; many times they are drunk or on drugs; perhaps mentally ill; and often with no-one else to turn to. Still others are homeless and asking for a bed. Some are very difficult to deal with—abusive, aggressive, unpredictable, with multiple and complex needs. Others, easy-going and appreciative, simply want the warmth of human company or a hot drink.

Experience Elsewhere
The picture outside the capital can be similar, though the cities tend to act like magnets drawing in the homeless and those most in need. On the larger housing estates, in towns where the main industry has gone, and in village and rural areas, callers may not come to the church door quite so often, but when they do, the needs can be just as great.

Different locations have different callers. In one area of the northwest of England, for instance, most callers at one particular rectory are gypsy 'Travellers' whose requests for help are punctuated with 'God bless you.' In more rural situations further help may not be to hand to call upon, the necessary back-up services either non-existent or many hours away.

There is a mythical media-generated picture of the church and in particular vicarage life that owes much to Victorian literature and such modern TV programmes as *Miss Marple*, the *Vicar of Dibley* and *Ballykissangel*. Whilst a few of these places might still exist, these pictures of Arcadian rural tranquillity are not the experience of most in ministry today.

3
Models for Care and Key Issues

'Knocking at Heaven's Door,' a conference held at The London Institute for Contemporary Christianity in 1994, attracted much interest across the London Diocese. The participants—men and women, ordained and lay—told their sometimes horrific personal stories and shared their concerns with the others present. This experience subsequently led to the formation of a London Diocesan working party, the publication of a nationally circulated report,[1] and much discussion within the wider church.

At the conference it was quite a revelation to find that though the belief in care was strong, years of practise had led many to withdraw from directly providing care altogether. Those who continued to do so frequently expressed feelings of ambivalence and guilt arising for a variety of reasons, not least the cost to family life. The care of some, they said, could be seen to cause the abuse of others.

Washing Feet

At the conference, participants accepted that Christians are called to serve where God calls them, but acknowledged that this was not necessarily easy or straightforward. Indeed, how are carers prepared for what they will experience? In John 13 we read of a definitive act of service when Jesus washed his disciples' feet and instructed them to do likewise.

A painting of this act of Christ hangs in the study of the Reverend Brian Lee, rector of St Botolph's in the City of London. For one who is responsible for a significant project for the homeless, this painting serves as a constant reminder and challenge; a supremely motivating model for the giving of Christ-like care. He says that it moves him and his team to care for London's many homeless.

Such a picture of a Lord who stoops to touch the smelly and the dirty in order to refresh and to cleanse, to refresh and restore, provides an ideal of care. But how does such a powerful model from a different time and culture actually translate into modern experience?

We need also to address the question whether we are to wash all the feet all the time, without discrimination or hesitation. This raises another question, that of managing and rationing care. This is an important issue, because those who are unable to manage the delivery of care may quickly find they provide something other than what they originally intended. Or they may have to give up providing care altogether.

---

[1] CARIS, *Knocking at Heaven's Door* (Diocese of London, 1996).

MODELS FOR CARE AND KEY ISSUES

Good Shepherds

As the first disciples watched Jesus washing their feet, their minds might well have gone back to his earlier words recorded in John 10 where Jesus said, 'I am the good shepherd. The good shepherd lays down his life for the sheep.' Perhaps, it might be argued, we are to spend and be spent in the service of our Lord without counting the cost. We are engaged in a costly self-sacrificial ministry. Faithful good shepherds do no less than this. Moving forward, what follows John 10 and John 13 is an even better known symbol of Christian service—the self-sacrificial love of Jesus going to the cross.

The Cross

How then might these powerful symbols of care—the washer of feet, the good shepherd whose sheep always come first and the giver of costly love as demonstrated by the Jesus dying on the cross—be grounded in the practice of Christian care today? Following Jesus in the way of the cross is a call to show love without limit.

Whilst holding fast to such a high ideal of love, we might ask ourselves in the light of our own weakness whether there are other, less demanding models of Jesus' love we can draw on. We might think that it is straightforward to care, simply to 'go to it,' but those who have been giving care for awhile say otherwise. How did the human side of Jesus cope with the demands of his ministry?

Learning to Care

Brian Lee says that Christians need to work out strategies for coping. This step is a necessary movement from belief to good practice. Just as starting to walk for a toddler is a bold adventure and there are many tumbles on the way, so it is for Christians who have to learn how to put faith into practice.

Those who wash feet also need time to rest and pray, for Jesus himself did not wash feet all the time. Those who care for sheep are no good as sleeping or dead shepherds. And though Christians may be called upon to lay down their lives in their service of Christ, they would be foolish to seek martyrdom or glory in doing so. A key theological question, then, addresses the nature and extent of care and whether care can be managed to ensure quality delivery.

Yes, Christians believe they ought to provide for the people who call, but what is involved practically in such encounters? What care can realistically be provided on the doorstep? Is advice enough, or is it possible to provide something more?

For instance, a recently married, young Christian youth worker said to me that he would never turn anyone away from his door who needed somewhere to sleep for the night. But what did his wife think? How would this affect his ministry to the young people he was working with? Indeed, what about the other people inevitably caught up in the church's ministry of care, such as the spouses and families, the church workers, the lodgers and visitors and the wider public? Ought not they be considered and if necessary protected?

Such concerns point toward a potential conflict of care between the needs of the caller and the needs of others. St Paul in his first letter to Timothy, chapter 3, questioned whether someone was fit to take on a position of responsibility and care within the church family if he did not first look after his own household. Paul's choice of words and use of the verbs 'manage' and 'look after' are significant here. Clearly, the qualities of managed care and leadership in one area are also needed in the other.

Health and Safety

In these changing times some think the attendance of clergy at rudimentary self-defence classes is an answer to the challenges of giving care. But these kind of literal knee-jerk responses, which have their place, can simply mask the need for a more considered response.

Thankfully, we live in an age when there is an increasing awareness of the importance of health and safety issues, and it is a sign of the times that this essentially caring legislation is now being worked out in relation to church life. Church ministers and their congregations are currently being asked to take on board the *House of Bishops' Policy on Child Protection*[2] and the Home Office *Safe from Harm*[3] guidelines for the protection of children.

Thus it is entirely appropriate that we in our churches should now consider how the doorstep encounter is safely and appropriately managed. It would be quite wrong to see these developments as the dead hand of an overprotective 'nanny' state or 'nanny' church. There can be little doubt that a proper concern for health and safety can help drive forward our thinking about providing appropriate care.

The Social Context of Callers

In recent decades the number of people who were once cared for within the secure restraining environment of the mental hospital has fallen dramatically as former patients are released into the community under the various provisions for community care. Sadly, many people have not successfully made the transition to settled life in the community and community care has remained a 'catch phrase' rather than become a reality.

Some of the mentally ill have become homeless and many are lonely. The most significant point of care in the community to meet their needs has been identified as the church. This means that the mentally ill are a specifically identifiable group who are increasingly presenting themselves at the church door in need of help. This is one group of callers where particular skills are required in meeting their needs.

---

[2] House of Bishops, *Policy on Child Protection* (Issued January 1999).
[3] Home Office, *Safe from Harm* (London: HMSO, 1993).

MODELS FOR CARE AND KEY ISSUES

Formulating Guidelines for Good Practice

Once one engages with the question of what might sensibly and safely be provided in the way of care, further questions and a raft of wider considerations soon arise. It may be that the provision of doorstep, off-the-street care may be handled better at some locations rather than others, by some people rather than others, within some premises rather than others, at certain times rather than others, and so on. And at those locations where it is agreed that care may take place, it may be prudent to draw up some specific operational guidelines, not only to outline what care is available but also to protect the people and resources directly linked with the provision of the care.

There are many people and places where quality care is presently given who employ considerable expertise. In London, for example, 'The Passage' in Victoria is a centre with an open-door policy that deals with hundreds of callers off the street each day. Staff there see caring for the caller as 'very specialist work.' They offer anything from a cheap cooked breakfast to help for those with mental-health problems. Whilst providing quality care to a high standard, the carers themselves are protected and supported by a list of carefully drawn up guidelines. This is far removed from the all-too-brief training once given to would-be clergy that simply saw ministry on the doorstep as 'time with angels.'

In Exeter there is another example of a creative response to the homeless, beggars and poor called 'The Palace Gates Project.' One of its several initiatives is a 'Food Voucher Scheme' that is being replicated in other parts of the country.

Whose Is Responsible to Care?

In the past, the common assumption was that all were equipped and gifted to provide care to callers. But this is patently not the case. The Bible speaks of gifts being given to the body of Christ—differing gifts for different people. As we look at any group of people we will see that some have the gifts and skills to care while others have gifts that lie elsewhere. St Paul describes the gifts being distributed so that some would be 'evangelists, some pastors and teachers' (Ephesians 4.11).

In general terms it is true to say all Christians are called to be good neighbours (see Luke 10.27), but sometimes what is required is more than warm neighbourliness, it is skilled specialist help. Whilst we in the churches might be able to provide some assistance, the solution to the problems may in fact not be ours.

Take the issue of homelessness, for example. In 1992 the Presidents of the Council of Churches of Britain and Ireland said, 'While we in the churches remain committed to "feeding the hungry" and "sheltering the homeless poor," it is Government and politicians who are ultimately responsible for developing long term viable solutions to a national problem which has reached crisis proportions.'

The scene then is set. A few examples of callers give a taste of the kind of problems that present themselves. Steve and Gary have needs that go far beyond what ordinary warm good-neighbourliness might be expected to address. In the face of such difficult callers, our belief in caring is not surprisingly tested. In particular places and for certain people, such as Sue, the burden of care is almost unbearable. How can the carer, the children of the carer's household, and the vulnerable in God's household be kept safe from harm? This is something not just for the minister, but for the whole church to think about.

A simple faith based upon the model of service, shepherding, and self-sacrifice provided by Jesus provides an ideal to which we can aspire. Yet the Bible also invites us to take a broader perspective and consider our other existing responsibilities toward those who have claims on our love and care. Experience seems to suggest that quality care can be best provided where it has been thought through, but in practice this is not always the case and care is quite often provided on an *ad hoc* basis. It gets left to one or two individuals.

I shall argue that both the provision of specialist skilled care and opportunistic spontaneous doorstep compassion have their place, but both need to be well managed and provided after sound guidelines have been considered. The remainder of this booklet examines these issues further.

4
Theology and the Provision of Care

> *Saviour and friend, how wonderful art Thou!*
> *My companion upon the changeful way.*
> *The comforter of its weariness.*
> *My guide to the eternal town.*
> *The welcome at its gate.*
>
> Alistair Maclean

We have already briefly uncovered some of the spiritual roots and motivation that Christians bring consciously or subconsciously to this issue. Primarily, Christians are motivated to care for others because Jesus Christ first loved them.

The Cross

On the cross Jesus let the full weight of the burden of sin rest on his shoulders, that he might make the supreme and once-for-all sacrifice. Thus the cross is the very ideal of sacrificial love, the Christian's most potent symbol. In the cross, all that had gone before—the Old Testament world with its patriarchs, priests and prophets—is superseded by a new revelation of God's love for all humanity made known in Jesus Christ. The meaning and reality of salvation is given new birth.

Along the journey of life, a Pentecostal companion in the Spirit has been given who will lead Christians all the way to the eternal city. A new deep path of love made explicit in the person and work of Jesus is made manifest through the continuing presence of the Holy Spirit given as a loving and helping person for the blessing and enabling of every believer.

'Love Your Neighbour'

Following the pattern set by Jesus, Christians continue to offer care to those in need. The hungry (Acts 2.7–30) are fed, and in fact the picture given of the early church is of a caring community who especially supported widows and orphans but who also gave 'as any had need' (Acts 2.45).

Jesus in his summary of the commandments endorsed God's instruction that we should love both God and our neighbour. As to the question, 'who is my neighbour?' he made it clear in the story of the Good Samaritan that the neighbour was any person in need who crosses our path (Luke 10.25–37). Just as the Samaritan helped the victim of crime at the roadside, so are we to 'go and do likewise.' Derek Tidball in his book *Skilful Shepherds*,[4] appealingly describes God's call for us to be a 'warm caring neighbour' to the one in need.

---

4   D Tidball, *Skilful Shepherds* (Leicester: IVP, 1986).

'Thy Kingdom Come'

In Matthew 25 the kingdom is promised to those who feed the hungry, give a drink to the thirsty, look after the sick, clothe the naked, and visit those in prison. Those who provide this care are told, 'just as you did it to one of the least of these who are members of my family, you did it to me' (v40).

Throughout its pages the Bible has many stories that commend a pattern of unconditional love. It also makes it clear that God has a special heart for the needs of the poor and those on the very margins of community life. Isaiah writes that God says "to let the oppressed go free ... to share your bread with the hungry, and bring the homeless poor into your house' (58.6, 7). Elsewhere in the Old Testament (see Leviticus 25.8–17 and Deuteronomy 15.1–11) we see God's pattern of Sabbath and Jubilee, designed to help people make a new start and escape from poverty. Arguably, because of God's provision in these ways, the poor in those days were more integrated in society than those on the streets of today.

Boundaries

This all raises important questions as to the boundaries in providing care. On the one hand, Christ's love is sacrificial unto death itself. There appears to be no boundary beyond which Christ-like love will not go. On the other hand, we are to note that Jesus in his own ministry set boundaries; he did not provide care on demand. Jesus took time out for his own rest and refreshment. Simon and his companions went to look for Jesus, and when they found him, they exclaimed, 'Everyone is searching for you!' Jesus replied, 'Let us go to the neighbouring towns' (Mark 1.36–38). Jesus was disciplined in the exercise of his care, making sure he recharged his own spiritual batteries.

Addressing the Key Relational and Practical Needs

Jesus used his own relationship with those he met to point them beyond their presenting problem to their core concerns. It was to these core concerns he then ministered skilfully. In John 4 we find that Jesus as he travelled north became tired and thirsty. He stopped to rest at Jacob's well and a woman came to draw water. Although the woman was in spiritual need of counsel and in physical need of water for her own use, Jesus first asked her to draw water for himself.

A relationship was built as the encounter developed and conversation flowed. As it did, Jesus used his encounter with the Samaritan woman to offer her more than she had bargained for. He offered her 'living water' and the forgiveness of her sins. He did not in so many words offer her a solution to her immediate pressing problem of having had five husbands plus the man she was currently living with. But he ministered to her deepest spiritual need, which opened the way for her to overcome the barrier between herself and God. In this he opened the way for her to begin to address her other life problems.

In building a pastoral relationship with this woman Jesus had to transcend all the political, religious and cultural taboos of his day while discerning her deepest concerns and needs. Today, Christian authors like Alistair Campbell emphasize a model of pastoral care where a certain quality of relationship is offered by the carer, a relationship marked by 'honesty, steadfastness, personal wholeness, mutuality, the courage of sacrificial love, vulnerability, folly, gracefulness, and a companionship which is more like being with people than doing things for them.'[5] The woman at the well had to go away and decide how then she would live. Jesus did not do everything for her, but opened up new possibilities in her life.

Handling Conflict

Beside choosing the locations and times when he would offer help, Jesus also made deliberate policy choices as to when and where he would face conflict. Sometimes he moved away from potential trouble and at other times he confronted it head on. In John 4, we read that Jesus led his disciples north from Judea to return to the relative safety of Galilee because his activities were being noticed by the Pharisees.

For us in situations of conflict with a caller, there is no special merit in escalating tension. This could simply lead to a greater risk of violence toward the carer, the caller and other people or property. However brief, a relationship forms at the door, and skill and discernment are needed to inform the outcome.

Vulnerability

St Paul in his letter to the Philippians (chapter 2) speaks volumes about vulnerability as he describes the way in which Jesus emptied himself of the glory of heaven to come to earth for our sake. We have considered the familiar call to be good shepherds who lay down their life for their sheep and carers who take up their crosses. But before we rush to offer ourselves on the pyre of self-sacrificial love, let us first think about whether we have considered all the biblical options.

Vanessa Herrick in *Limits of Vulnerability* helpfully explores this issue as it is applied to pastoral ministry. She acknowledges the value of the 'gift' of vulnerability, but adds, 'such a chosen vulnerability will neither be appropriate to every pastoral encounter, nor in every context.'[6]

Compromised pastors, injured ministers, or those who have been 'disabled' at the door may end up unable to fulfil obligations of love either to family or church. Alternative approaches to pastoral care at the door may be preferable. It may well be that the gifts are exercised through someone else to deliver this ministry of care.

Differing Gifts, Separate Roles

The apostles in the early church themselves soon found that they needed to organize a separation of duties so that some might teach and others might exercise pastoral care. In Acts 6 we read of the recruitment of extra believers to help

---

5 A Campbell, *Rediscovering Pastoral Care* (London: DLT, 1981).
6 V Herrick, *Limits of Vulnerability* (Grove Pastoral Series No 71, Cambridge: Grove Books Ltd, 1997), p. 23.

with the distribution to the poor. It is clear that the Bible sees people having different gifts. The gift of providing pastoral care is not given to all, though to be a warm caring neighbour is.

The problems and difficulties presented by callers can be so complex that the caller's needs may best be served by linking them with the person who can best serve their need. A working church is one where the different members are each using their separate gifts to build up the body, and this seems to counter the popular assumption that the one ministering always has to be the church leader.

Carers are called to bring the love of Christ to bear upon the needs of the caller. They do so as a warm, caring neighbour. But that does not mean to say that they will ultimately be the person best placed to deliver the 'deep' care the caller may need. Let us turn now to consider in more detail the kind of pastoral needs that typically arise at the church, vicarage, presbytery or manse door.

5
Care in Practice

The rabbi asked his son...' Where does God live?'...
'Surely,' said the child, 'he fills the heaven and the earth?'
'No,' said the rabbi. 'God lives wherever we let him in.'

Jonathan Sacks

The Callers and Their Needs

All manner of people with their various needs call and present themselves before us. From time to time those who have come to my door have variously been in need of urgent medical help, in one case to save an infected arm from possible amputation. Another person, like a modern day leper, needed to talk because he was suffering with Aids.

The mentally ill call, sometimes for help with practical difficulties, sometimes because they just need someone to talk to. The needs of the mentally ill can vary enormously. One woman asked for help with a housing transfer. Or a mentally ill man who had not been receiving his medication for schizophrenia came to the door to tell me about the voices of men saying unpleasant things about him, voices that were being broadcast from the roof of every nearby building.

'Please can I have some water or a cup of tea?' is a common request. But other occasions have brought the unexpected demands of people asking me to provide help to arrange accommodation for the night. Or someone wanted a short-term loan to get electricity for cooking so the children can have a warm meal. Or I am asked whether I could provide the fare to get to work, college or home; for the deposit on a flat; for food; and so on. These are more often than not the opening lines in a bid to obtain easy cash for some addiction.

A lonely homosexual man repeatedly calls who is not easy to deal with. In fact, in the past he has made advances toward our children. Another man needed clothes and was found a pair of suitable trousers for when he called back the following week. Yet another caller, bottle of Scotch in his hand, wanted me to celebrate his birthday with him.

Some callers are potentially dangerous. One young man was armed and asking for 'sanctuary' as he was running away from the police. Another who had been involved in a serious crime and had served time in custody now regretted what he had done and came to ask me to hear his confession and pronounce absolution.

Sometimes callers ask for casual work and a small amount of cash for their trouble. Others are more forthright about their needs for money, and some weave wonderful tales of woe to secure financial help. Recently a man called in tears to say his only son had been killed in civil war in his native land. Even now his body remained unburied in a mortuary, and today the man's wallet had gone missing so he could not get to work that evening. Of course he did not want money from me, just a loan which he would repay the following Monday. He never did repay it, and I never saw him again.

But I have to remind myself that once before I helped a man with a similar, if less extreme tale of woe, and he came back to return the money I had given him. It was a deeply meaningful moment both for of us. Seneca once said, 'The most grievous kind of destitution is to want money in the midst of wealth.' Often Christians are called upon for money.

For the most part, callers have been placid, only sometimes assertive and demanding, and just occasionally aggressive. But the latter leave the lasting memories and raise the most concern. One woman demanded entry into the vicarage and tried to get in using force, refusing to accept there was no-one there at the time. Our teenage son who was alone in the vicarage at the time managed to force her outside and close the door. Occasionally, those who provide care are assaulted, tied up, abused, harmed or very occasionally killed.

Multi-problem Lives

In general the lives of callers are beset with multifaceted problems. Their quality of life and health is often poor. They are often lonely, marginalized, abused, illiterate, sick and exploited. They do not fit in with mainstream society. A survey carried out in London by a church-working party found that callers were asking for money (40%), food (25%), to chat (15%), clothing (8%), accommodation (8%), and other requests (4%). These were their presenting needs, and it was often self-evident that behind these practical requests lay major pastoral concerns, such as possibly as many as a third having alcohol and drug dependency problems.

A very real link has been established between those begging for money in London and homelessness. For instance, a 'Crisis' survey found that of the people begging on London's streets, some 80% had been homeless the previous night.[7] In London, these are likely to be the same people who are calling at the church door for help.

Clearly local situations differ and what is typical in central London will be different to what happens in the suburbs. Again, what happens in the capital city may not be the same as what happens in other cities, and what happens in urban centres will be different to the picture in the countryside. A local survey in one's own setting is relatively easy and inexpensive to conduct. It will provide invaluable information for understanding the local situation when planning a strategy.

Where a relationship with a caller leads to someone becoming part of a worshipping congregation, the needs of that person can have a serious pastoral impact. In times past our church used to be opposite an epileptic hospital, and so the church congregation were familiar with the patients sometimes having fits whilst in church. As epilepsy is now treated with drugs, the hospital has closed.

---

[7] A Murdoch, *We Are Human Too* (London: Crisis, 1994).

But other people who unexpectedly call occasionally make their presence known in the congregation. A man who had been sleeping rough came into church for the warmth, sat next to the heater and lit up a cigarette. He was told by a member of the congregation that smoking was not allowed. Other callers have come into church to ask the congregation for money.

Some members of the congregation have a history of hospitalization for mental illness. They have on the whole been accepted and warmly befriended, but this too has not always been easy. An unsolicited telephone call from the local Social Services warned the minister of the unstable mental state of one person in the congregation and the corresponding risk of violence.

Most of the problems of the caller cannot be 'solved' across a doorstep. An individual's problems have to be seen in terms of the wider social context, where social structures, conditions, and policy contribute to the situation of the caller. The way the benefits system works, the way housing policies operate, the opening and closing hours of welfare agencies and the treatment of refugees under the law are but four examples.

To hear an 'individual story' at the door may require reinterpretation so that the wider 'community story' can be heard and addressed. The encounter at the door often means rubbing shoulders with the raw edge of life, those on the margins of 'affluent' society, which can be uncomfortable. We are meeting the negative polarities in our society and the unforeseen consequences of social policy right at one's own front door when many people would prefer to believe only in a 'civilized' and 'successful' Britain.

The carers who were questioned in the course of the London survey raised important concerns of their own; of 'con men doing the rounds'; of the 'lack of information' they had to make available to callers; of their concern for their own security and that of others who may be vulnerable and at risk from callers. Carers felt they had a responsibility to be good stewards of the resources available to them, and they would like to have the necessary information about resources available elsewhere. These are questions to do with handling the delivery of care, and it is to the world of the carer that we now turn.

6
Care for Carers

In summary: facilitate a self-awareness and an increased inner strength that will allow us to take care of ourselves, not just others, and to become reasonably good parents to ourselves.
Mary Ann Coate

There can be few more pressing needs in the church of today than the provision of adequate and appropriate support for those called to the ordained ministry.
David Shepherd

Caring for ourselves as carers and finding the support needed for ministering to callers is a wide issue. It addresses something much bigger than simply helping us cope with the needs of callers at our door, as important as that is.

Carers in the Front Line

Wanda Nash in *Living with God at the Vicarage*[8] asked clergy and their wives (today we would refer to 'clergy and their spouses'), what caused them significant stress. Again the question considers a wider issue than our immediate concern, but the replies are relevant. They reported, 'We are just about the only people left who are on 24-hour call to the public. The call may be trivial or it may be important. How can one tell? We can never not answer the phone or the door.'

Wanda Nash's list of reported stress tells of invaded privacy, insecurity, the supply of care being used up by the carer so that there is none left for those in the family, other people's worries invading the home, being public, having an open door when one does not feel like it, not having a home of one's own, not being able to shut the door like other people can, exposing one's children to the tears of adults, carrying the burden of other people's problems and so on. The list seems to describe exactly what stress arises when handling callers at the door.

The clergy for their part reported the stress created by a lack of boundaries on time; that is, having an open-ended job where work just goes on and on. The little time they had was being interrupted, creating an unacceptable invasion of personal space. Again, these selected responses indicate the nature of the stress placed on those dealing with callers.

The London Diocesan survey received reports from some clergy and their spouses as to what they saw as 'intolerable circumstances under which they live and work.' This arose not only from being in certain locations of especial difficulty but also to a change in today's society. There were, it was said, times in the

---

8 W Nash, *Living with God at the Vicarage* (Grove Pastoral Series No 42, Cambridge: Grove Books Ltd, 1990).

past when the church, its clergy and their household were treated with respect. Today there has been a decline in that respect.

One clergy family, for example, wrote of how they had suffered 13 burglaries, adding that they felt there was a need for their diocese to provide *them* with care. Another clergy wife described how, clutching a young child in her arms, she had been forced to run from her home in panic after a man she had allowed in to use the toilet locked himself in. Callers at our own front door have sworn at and abused my wife, children and myself.

Yet there is also a strongly positive side to the ministry at the door, a ministry that elicits compassion, love and warmth, and the satisfaction that comes from relating with a fellow human in their time of need. Feeding the hungry, giving a cup of tea, providing clothing, giving directions to shelter and having a sympathetic ear are of immense value to those on the receiving end. Indeed, these are reasons why so many people turn to the church when in need.

In the Church of England, new incumbents are asked by the bishop instituting them, 'Will you care for the people of this parish in the name of Christ ... all who come in search of God's grace. Will you serve them with joy?' This, the only job description the new incumbent will get, is a calling that is both a privilege and a responsibility. With it comes accommodation, not down the road, not above the shop, but *in* the shop. And there is an invisible notice outside that says, 'open 24 hours a day, seven days a week.'

Sometimes the experience of ministering to callers generates not a positive attitude, but feelings of resentment, inadequacy, fear, anger, guilt, terror, isolation, loss and even panic. On occasion carers and their families have been placed at risk, and sadly some have suffered lasting consequences.

The households of those in ministry do face risks to their health and safety, and in some places the risk may be a considerable one. For historical reasons and lack of good property management, the homes of those in ministry can be isolated buildings where it is not easy to summon help and where families can be left feeling very exposed, isolated and vulnerable. For this reason some clergy make an impassioned plea to live in ordinary homes in ordinary streets.

All Carers

I have given a lot of space to the needs of those in the front line, but the ministry of care is not solely located with the minister or the minister's family. People at church, those running projects, working with the homeless, providing a counselling service, or whatever, also need support and supervision. They will need to agree boundaries and learn how to care for themselves. And a wider group of people in the church will need to ensure they are receiving appropriate support.

For example, doorstep care should concern the archdeacons and diocesan parsonage committees who consider the location, nature and facilities provided for minister's housing, the parish office and other public church buildings. It also concerns the support networks in place to ensure that pastoral support is offered and taken up.

7
Limits of Care

I had a dream that I was in heaven knocking at the door of the shop of spiritual gifts. 'I need all the fruit of the Spirit you can sell me,' I said, 'that I may help a young man at my front door.' The angel replied, 'we sell seeds, not fruit; and besides, no customer may take all the seeds, but just what we give them.'

With apologies to Leslie Hunter

We, who are many, are one body in Christ, and individually we are members one of another. We have gifts that differ according to the grace given to us.

Romans 12.5–6

Seeds, not Fruit

It is both a comfort and a worry to know that we are given seeds from which fruit will come. Sometimes we are tempted to think we have been given all the gifts, fully to hand, for all the people. But this is not the case. We may get things wrong; we may fail; we may not nurture and exercise the gifts we have been given as we should.

I find it reassuring to think of the gifts in seed form, for it reminds me that the Lord knows our limitations and weaknesses and he forgives us. We are always learners and wounded healers, taking one call after another, ministering to one caller after another, and hopefully maturing to bear fruit as time goes by. Some seeds and indeed fruit will not be ours, for others will have gifts that we do not possess. We need to be ready to turn to, enable, and involve them in their ministry.

I Need Too

As we mature and grow in Christ, we will exercise the responsibility toward ourselves to watch over and look after ourselves. This is not being selfish, for our Lord himself took time out to go into the desert to be with his Father and to pray. He needed to rest and be refreshed. At one time he slept in a boat when he was tired, though those around him needed him awake. He took time not just to heal but to support the band of people he gathered round himself. There are times when we try and help when we have not got the skills, doing so out of a blind but sincere sense of needing to care.

Accepting our Limitations

There are times when we get it wrong and may realize only after someone has gone from the doorstep that we have been conned. A colleague may tell of the same tale of woeful misfortune that we have heard word for word at our own front door only that morning. Once, for instance, thinking I was wise in providing a public transport ticket rather than cash, I discovered that down at the at the local pub the ticket had been sold and turned into liquid assets.

Accepting that we are sometimes fools for Christ helps. One clergyman has given away his life savings to a caller at his door. Whether such self-sacrifice was appropriate or not is not easily judged—God alone knows. Help at the door can be as much an art form as a precise science. It also helps if we do not take ourselves too seriously, if we can laugh at our own gullibility and the situation comedy that so often arises.

We Are Part of a Body
The Bible teaches us that we are part of a body, the people of God, and that the gifts are distributed not to one person but to the various members of the body. Often the church assumes that all the gifts and responsibilities of pastoral care rest with the minister.

Why is it that so often the ministers see themselves as the sole focus for giving care? Is it reasonable to expect a minister (or anyone else) to be available at all times, night and day? Is the minister setting realistic boundaries as to what is reasonable and safe, and then keeping to them? And is it always necessary that the pastoral care be carried out from home? These are the kind of questions ministers, their households and their church congregations need to ask.

God Has No Limitations; We Are Limited
Because we are limited, it is helpful to ask what level of need there is and what kind of service we can realistically offer the caller at the door. It seems a sensible precaution not to let total strangers into one's home, nor to let vulnerable members of the minister's household or church deal with callers at the door. It is probably good practice not to give money.

Callers find it helpful to know quickly what is and is not available, and it is sensible to have a consistent set of rules about this. Whenever anyone calls, it is important that callers never go away feeling rejected or unloved. Even when the thing they ask for is not available, we can usually find some way to make the encounter positive.

The Benefits of Christians Working Together
Churches often find that they can best serve the needs of callers by working together and having a local strategy. Pooling gifts and resources tends to lead to a better provision, and even to the creation of centres of excellence. Some churches have a care scheme and can cope with callers.

Partnerships with other voluntary and statutory bodies can be fruitful. It is good to know where such projects are and how to refer people to them. Good practice where the needs of the carer and the callers are appropriately and safely attended to are often easier to achieve where a co-operative effort has been made. A group of people with the necessary skills can be brought together, rather than one person in isolation meeting the need.

There are many such places up and running. In the centre of London, for example, there are places where a whole platform of care is provided for those who call (including counselling, chiropody, and so on). And a cheap but wholesome cooked breakfast is available each day at 'The Passage' in Victoria. Thus it is not necessary for any single local church to lay on such services.

There generally is more available to people on the street in the city centres than in the outer suburbs, but this may not be so everywhere. The Enfield Churches in North London work together to provide a drop-in centre for Refugees and Asylum Seekers. Food, counselling and some help with fares may be given. With the help of a number of churches the Salvation Army provide a regular soup-and-sandwich run to London's homeless, also offering blankets and clothing. At our own church, certain harvest gifts are kept by in a special box to provide food for the hungry who call. And it is the practice of many churches to provide a small discretionary fund to those who give pastoral care to callers for when needs arise.

In North London, the churches together (ECSRA), as elsewhere in the country, have produced a printed information list of useful agencies. These addresses and telephone numbers have been circulated to all local ministers to be available for when callers knock. Included is information regarding local night-shelters, Alcoholics Anonymous, the benefits office, homeless units, social services, hospitals, drop-in centres, Cruse and Relate.

Practical Help or Advice Only?

Should one decide to offer more at the front door than just advice and information, some useful guidelines can be followed. For example, it is useful to keep a note of the 'stories' people tell. Patterns emerge and these stories can be useful in putting together a picture of local need.

When callers knock, it is helpful for them to know whether their demand is unreasonable. It is also quite appropriate to ask a caller to come back at a more convenient time. Remember, meeting callers' needs on demand often means treating other people less well in the time previously allocated to them. It is always good practice to manage the caller rather than to make a knee-jerk response that drops everything and everyone else.

With a bit of proactive planning it may be possible to secure the services of a local café or shop that will provide items on your authority that you can then pay for later. This overcomes some of the worry we have about giving money that might be spent on alcohol or drugs. But some callers seem able to trade whatever is given for cash.

Following are a few strategies and guidelines for the mutual benefit of both callers and carers.

Appendix
Guidelines for Practice

1. Care

The writer of Ecclesiastes observed, 'Like fish taken in a cruel net ... so mortals are snared at a time of calamity, when it suddenly falls upon them' (9.12). Perhaps the first thing to consider when a caller comes is that 'there but for the grace of God stand I." The once commonly held Victorian approach to social responsibility—passing moral judgment and attaching blame to those suffering misfortune—still conditions the thinking of many in the church. Instead, our first step is to see the caller through the eyes of Christ, who said, 'In everything do to others as you would have them do to you' (Matthew 7.12).

2. Prayer

The next thing we can do is to pray. It may be an arrow prayer with the person before us at the door, or it may be that the concerns and needs of the individual callers elicit and inform rather more considered prayer later. Indeed, it may be that the person calling would like prayers offered by you with them. On occasion I have received callers who have specifically asked for a prayer or a blessing.

3. Decide the Level of Care Available at Your Door

Are you gifted, resourced, and available to safely provide more than an information-only service to callers? Assess your gifts, and once these are identified, stick within the limits of the service you can provide.

4. Information Only

If an information-only service is your limit, then:
a) Ensure no caller leaves feeling rejected or unloved.
b) Apply consistent rules, and quickly let the caller know what you can and cannot offer them.
c) Be ready to give useful information relating to other sources of help locally. Have them easily available to give to the caller.
d) Consult with others. Share stories and work to provide together what no one person or church could do alone.
e) Know where to refer a pastoral counselling need.
f) Keep the person safely on the other side of the door.

5. Providing More than Information:
a) Maintain a stock of food and drinks that can be handed out, perhaps through harvest produce. Organize a food voucher system with a local shop or café.
b) Set times and boundaries as to availability.

c) Note and share the stories people tell, and use them to shape policy and action.
d) Help callers to get to the point.
e) Refer people to appropriate specialist caring agencies.
f) Provide a cup of tea and a sandwich, and have a caring listening ear. Such provision has a good track record in the church.
g) Do not look for thanks.
h) Generally refuse the requests for money, but know when to use discretion.

6. Wider Questions

We need to ask questions about the issues that callers coming to our door raise. These should be considered not only by the person who opens the door, but also for the wider church. In the past perhaps it was the usual practice to see one or two people in the local church providing care. Where this still happens, and it does, (sometimes quite appropriately), the experience of the carer(s) might be usefully reviewed by the congregation or its church council. Questions to consider might include:

- safety of individual carers and their families;
- ability and competence to provide the required service;
- back-up support available;
- suitability and safety of the premises for such encounters;
- working with others.

Romans 12.5–6 seems an appropriate point at which to end, for it reminds us of our common belonging to one another as parts of the body of Christ. As the carer acts for us all in caring for the caller, so the carer and those others closely involved need in turn to receive the care of the whole body of Christ.